Raiders and Conquerors

Written by A.N. George
Illustrated by David McAllister

MARKS & SPENCER

Marks and Spencer p.l.c.
Baker Street, London W1U 8EP
www.marksandspencer.com

This book was created by Monkey Puzzle Media Ltd

ISBN 1-84273-343-5

Printed in Dubai, U.A.E.

Designer: Victoria Webb
Editor: Jason Hook
Artwork commissioning:
Roger Goddard-Coote
Project manager: Alex Edmonds

Contents

Who were the first British settlers?

OVER 500,000 YEARS AGO, PREHISTORIC HUMANS STARTED TO MIGRATE from Europe to Britain. They were hunters who wandered around the land looking for animals like sabre-toothed tigers, oxen and deer. These early people belonged to a species called *Homo erectus* (which means upright human being). You could say they were the first people to conquer Britain.

Did the first settlers sail to Britain?

No, they walked! The seas were much lower in prehistoric times, and Britain was not an island. There was no need for the Channel Tunnel as Britain was still connected by land to the European continent.

How was the land conquered?

Around 8500 BC more settlers arrived from Europe. They were farmers who brought with them seeds for growing barley and wheat. They settled mostly in the south and east of England, as well as in Scotland and Ireland. Over the years, they cleared much of Britain's forests. The wild land had been conquered by humans.

Who was *Homo sapiens*?

Over 230,000 years ago a new species of human replaced *Homo erectus*. Called *Homo sapiens* (wise human being) they were more intelligent than their predecessors and knew how to build shelters from wood and animal bones. These early humans were very different to us, but we do have something in common with them – we belong to the same species. We are all *Homo sapiens*!

Early Britons building huts.

Where did the Celts come from?

BY 500 BC, FIERCE, WARLIKE PEOPLE were finding their way to Britain. They were called Celts, and they came from central Europe. They travelled around the region and gradually became the main race of people in France, Germany, Spain and Britain.

Celts feasting.

How did the Celts change life in Britain?
When the Celts first came to Britain, people lived in small villages surrounded by the fields they farmed. Soon, however, the small villages grew into tribal areas. Each tribe had its own king and queen. Neighbouring tribes made war on each other and there were fierce battles.

What was a druid?
The Celts had priests called druids. They organized religious festivals, during which they cut mistletoe with golden sickles. Some disagreements between tribes of Celts were settled by these mysterious druids. Although they did not take part in battles, they shared in the spoils of war.

How did the Celts bleach their hair?
Many Celts used lime to bleach and stiffen their blonde hair, then combed it back from their foreheads to give it the appearance of a horse's mane. Officers of high rank used to grow big moustaches too. They believed this gave them a dignified appearance.

Why did the Celts smell so good?
The Celts were proud of their cleanliness, and used soaps and perfumes. They were also proud of their appearance: they liked to wear brightly coloured shirts; special trousers known as bracae; and enormous cloaks with checked or stripy designs, draped over their shoulders and fastened with beautiful brooches of gold or silver.

NAKED FURY

The Celts were a frightening sight in battle. They preferred to fight stark naked – except for their favourite golden armlets and a ring around their necks called a torc. Huge horns were played during a fight, and the naked warriors sang songs and screamed to frighten their enemy.

When did the Romans conquer Britain?

IN 55 BC, THE ROMAN GENERAL JULIUS CAESAR WAS ATTEMPTING TO conquer France. The British Celts, or Britons, rushed to help their neighbours, and an angry Caesar swore revenge. After France was captured, he turned his attention to Britain, but fierce storms in the English Channel drove the Roman ships away. It was not until AD 43 that the Romans made another serious attempt to conquer Britain. That year 40,000 Roman troops launched a successful invasion, and Britain became Britannia – a Roman colony.

Which queen found the Romans taxing?
Although some tribes of Celts co-operated with the Romans, most fought back against the invaders. One tribe called the Iceni was ruled by a famous warrior queen called Boudicca. She led a rebellion against the Romans in AD 60 after they had demanded the Iceni pay heavy taxes. But the rebellion was crushed, and Boudicca killed herself by taking poison.

What was life like in Roman Britain?
The Romans built large towns and introduced a lifestyle that was amazingly modern. Towns contained a main square where there were shops, workshops, offices and law courts. The square was also used as a market, where Britons could buy things they had never seen before – including apples, onions, olives, grapes and oysters.

How did the Romans roam?
Before the Romans arrived, Britain's only roads were dirt tracks. To make it easier for their army to travel round the country, the Romans built 16, 000 kilometres of excellent roads, wonderfully straight and constructed from three layers of stones and grit. They also built inns and forts where weary travellers could rest for the night and get a bite to eat.

Who was worth their salt?
Sometimes Roman soldiers were given salt as part of their wages. This was known as salarium, from which we get the word 'salary'.

Could anyone become a Roman soldier?
Ancient Rome was a truly multi-cultural society. Anyone from a conquered country could join the army. They could even rise to become emperor – the famous emperor Septimus Severus was Libyan. When foreign soldiers retired from the army, they were given Roman citizenship.

Who borrowed their gods?
The Romans borrowed many of their gods from the Greeks, but gave them new names. Roman soldiers also worshipped foreign gods they had discovered during campaigns abroad. One of the most popular was the Persian god Mithras.

Why did the Romans leave Britain?
By AD 300, the Roman Empire was so vast it was becoming impossible for the army to patrol all of its borders. Enemies raided Roman settlements throughout north-east Europe. Tribes called Picts and the Scots were overrunning northern Britain, and Saxon marauders attacked from the south. By AD 410 the army was needed to defend Rome, and Britain was left to fend for itself.

HADRIAN BUILDS WONDER WALL

In AD 122, the emperor Hadrian ordered his soldiers to build a massive wall across the north of Britain, to prevent an invasion by barbarian tribes that lived there. Hadrian's Wall took six years to complete and was 117 km long. The ruins of the wondrous wall can still be seen today.

How good was the Roman army?

Roman soldiers on the march.

FOR HUNDREDS OF YEARS, THE ROMAN ARMY WAS THE BEST IN THE WORLD.

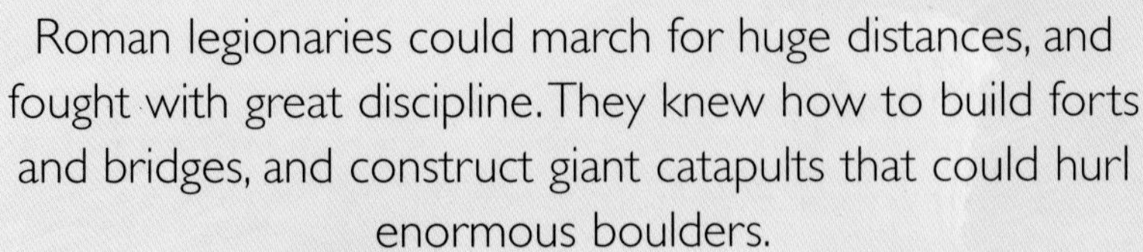
Roman legionaries could march for huge distances, and fought with great discipline. They knew how to build forts and bridges, and construct giant catapults that could hurl enormous boulders.

Roman soldiers building Hadrian's Wall.

Who were the Anglo-Saxons?

THE ANGLES, SAXONS AND JUTES WERE EUROPEAN TRIBES THAT SPOKE A German language. They came from territories that are now in Holland, southern Denmark and West Germany. After the Romans left, these tribes made more and more raids on the south coast of Britain. At first, they returned home after each attack, but gradually they decided to settle. The new arrivals mixed together and became known as Anglo-Saxons.

An Anglo-Saxon thane.

Why were the Anglo-Saxons invited?

By AD 430, most Britons were under the rule of a warlord named Prince Vortigern. Facing attack from marauding tribes of Picts and Scots, Vortigern invited Anglo-Saxon warriors to come and fight on his side. There was no problem getting them to come, but more of a problem getting them to leave. They liked the country so much they stayed! These fierce Anglo-Saxons claimed vast areas of land for themselves.

Who were Hengist and Horsa?

In 455, Vortigern's new Anglo-Saxon friends turned on him. He was defeated in battle by the brothers Hengist and Horsa, and an Anglo-Saxon kingdom was established in Kent. By 491 the Anglo-Saxons had control of the south coast, and by 600 they ruled the whole of England.

What does England mean?

The word England comes from an Anglo-Saxon word meaning 'land of the Angles'. This referred to the people called Angles, rather than suggesting that England had funny shaped hills!

Who was the first king of England?

Anglo-Saxon settlements united themselves into seven different kingdoms, called Kent, East Anglia, Sussex, Essex, Wessex, Mercia and Northumbria. The kingdoms were ruled by different leaders who fought to gain control of each others' territories. By 757, King Offa of Mercia had become ruler of all the kingdoms – the first true king of England.

What were churls and thanes?

At the top of Anglo-Saxon society were the thanes, the lords who owned all the land. They rented land to farmers called churls, who had to grow enough to keep their families and pay the thane. Even worse off than the churls were the poor slaves, who depended on their masters for food and lodgings.

King Arthur leads his men into battle.

Did King Arthur really exist?

NOBODY KNOWS FOR SURE WHO INSPIRED THE LEGEND OF King Arthur. But it may have been Owain Ddantgwyn, a warlord who led the Britons in glorious battles against the Anglo-Saxons. His headquarters were in a disused Roman fort in Wales, called Caerleon. This fort may have inspired the legend of Camelot, where the knights of King Arthur met at a round table.

BEOWULF SLAYS A DRAGON

The early Anglo-Saxons had a rich tradition of story-telling, but they could not write. When they settled in Britain they learnt Latin – and wrote down some of their beautiful stories. One of the most famous is the poem Beowulf, the first great work of English literature. It tells of the heroic warrior Beowulf, who fights with monsters and fire-breathing dragons.

Did the Anglo-Saxons have holidays?

People in Anglo-Saxon times celebrated eight major 'holy days', or holidays, every year. They had celebrations for such times as the planting of seeds and midsummer's night. At harvest time, children made corn dollies – a tradition that has lasted to the present day.

How was Yule celebrated?

Yule was a twelve-day celebration during which the Anglo-Saxons burnt a Yule Log in honour of the coming of spring. This custom survived into Christian times, when it became a Christmas tradition. Yule is now another word for Christmas.

Who were the Vikings?

THE VIKINGS WERE FARMERS FROM SWEDEN, NORWAY AND Denmark, who became known for seafaring and piracy. In summer, while Viking women and older men looked after the farms, the young men set off on their ships to pillage and loot. Their warriors believed that bravery was the greatest talent a man could have. The highest mark of respect in Viking society was having an epic poem written about your brave deeds. Poetry was very important to the Vikings – it was the way they recorded their history.

When did the Vikings conquer Britain?
In 787, three mysterious ships approached the coast of southern England. From them rushed bloodthirsty warriors, who looted and burned coastal settlements then sailed away over the horizon. It was the first of many Viking attacks that terrorized England, and soon the raiders were coming not to raid but to conquer. By 850, the Vikings had built forts down the east coast of Britain from the Orkneys to the Thames. In 865, they attacked and conquered Mercia, East Anglia and parts of Northumbria. The Vikings were here to stay.

Who tried greatly to stop the Viking invasion?
Alfred the Great led Saxon attempts to fight off the Viking invasion. The king himself designed new ships with high sides that could withstand Viking arrows. After Alfred won battles against the Vikings, they retreated into territory north of London – which became known as the Danelaw.

How did Cnut make waves?
By 1017, a wise Viking called Cnut had become the undisputed king of England. He became famous for standing on a beach and ordering the waves to stop advancing. This was not a foolish act of vanity but an attempt by Cnut to show his people that you cannot stop the inevitable from happening.

What did the Vikings do with dragons?
They carved dragons out of wood, and used them to decorate their ships: a dragon's head at the prow, and a dragon's tail or a smaller head at the stern. The Vikings considered their ships, which they called longships, to be their most important possessions.

A raiding party of Vikings pillage and burn a settlement in England.

A Viking longship.

How did the Vikings build their longships?

A VIKING FIRST FELLED SOME OAK AND ASH TREES AND STORED THE TIMBER in shady woodland to season it. Prayers were said before the ship was built. The finished longship was painted over with a tar made by roasting pine-logs over a slow fire and collecting the resin as it oozed out. Sails were made from striped linen.

VIKINGS SCARED OF GHOSTS

When a Viking died, relatives did not carry the body out through the door. Instead they passed it through a hole in the wall which was immediately closed up again. This was meant to confuse the ghost of the dead person, so it could not find its way back into the house. During a funeral, Vikings disguised themselves by blackening their faces. This way, the ghost of the deceased would not recognize them and decide to haunt their home.

Why was Leif unlucky?
Vikings led by a man called Leif the Lucky managed to sail all the way from their settlement in Greenland to North America. Leif and his people settled on the east coast, but then Leif's luck ran out – Native Americans killed all his people's cattle and they had to sail home to Greenland.

What was at the end of the rainbow?
The Vikings worshipped a number of gods, whose father, or chief god, was Odin. They believed that a rainbow was a bridge that connected earth with the halls of Odin in the sky. If warriors fought bravely, they would be allowed to travel along the rainbow and join their gods for a never-ending feast.

Have you sung a Viking song?
Possibly – many playground songs can be traced back to the Vikings. These include In and Out the Windows and Walney Echoes, One, Two, Three. Many place names around the country are also of Viking origin, such as Whitby and Skegness.

Who was William of Normandy?

WILLIAM THE CONQUEROR WAS BORN IN FRANCE IN 1027, AND AT THE age of seven became Duke of Normandy. When he grew up he claimed that the English king Edward the Confessor, who was a cousin of William's father, had promised him he would inherit the English throne. William's French subjects considered him intelligent and fair, but not surprisingly they also thought he was very ambitious.

How did the French conquer England?
When Edward the Confessor died in January 1066, William of Normandy did not inherit the English throne. Instead, Harold Godwinson was crowned king. William was furious and sailed with his troops to Pevensey on the south coast of England. Harold's followers had just returned from the north, where they had defeated a Viking invasion, and were too weary to fight properly. They were massacred at the Battle of Hastings, and Harold was killed. England now had French rulers.

Were the English nobles loyal?
Sort of. When Harold was crowned king, they swore an oath of loyalty to him. Then when William the Conqueror was crowned King of England on Christmas Day 1066 at Westminster Abbey – they swore an oath of loyalty to him as well!

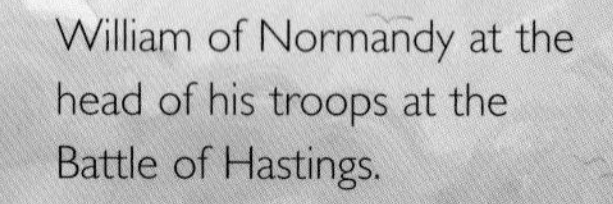
William of Normandy at the head of his troops at the Battle of Hastings.

How did the Normans rule England?
William the Conqueror brought no ordinary French people to live in England, only an army of 10,000 soldiers led by a handful of nobles. They were expected to rule over a population of 2 million English people – who did not like them very much! So they built castles throughout the land, and ruled from these powerful strongholds.

ONE IN THE EYE FOR HAROLD

The beautiful Bayeux Tapestry records the Norman Conquest in pictures. It shows a soldier plucking an arrow from his eye at the Battle of Hastings, and some historians believe this is Harold. Others claim Harold was killed by four soldiers – one pierced his chest with a lance; a second cut off his head with a sword; a third thrust a javelin into his belly; a fourth cut off his leg. It makes the arrow in the eye sound quite painless!

Did people go hunting in Norman times?

IN ANGLO-SAXON TIMES, POOR PEOPLE RELIED ON HUNTING FOR THEIR food, especially in years when the crops failed. But William seized a lot of land and turned it into 'royal forest'. When poor people continued to hunt on the king's land, they were arrested as poachers.

What was the Domesday Book?
The Domesday Book was a survey carried out by the Normans to record who owned the land and property in England. By the time it was finished in 1086, the great book recorded that over fifty castles had been built throughout the country.

Did life change for the English under Norman rule?
Yes, William removed the English earls and put his own barons in charge of estates dotted around the country. French barons controlled the estates, and rented out the land to English villagers. New laws required workers to live and work on one estate, which they were forbidden to leave.

How were poachers punished?
Punishment for poaching was severe. Stealing deer might be punished by the loss of an eye or a hand. Repeat offending (which was more difficult with only one eye or hand) could be punished by death.

Why did dogs lose their claws?
Some barons ordered the peasants' dogs to have the nails removed from their front paws so that they could not be used for hunting. No wonder there were uprisings in Kent, Wales, the West Country and the north of England.

What sport was played in Norman times?
Some people were fond of an early form of cricket, which they played with wooden or leather balls. The bats were curved sticks called 'crics', an Anglo-Saxon word for a shepherd's crook. Players stood in front of a wicket-gate while others hurled the ball to hit a cross-piece called a 'bail'.

In East Anglia, a noble by the name of Hereward the Wake made a stand against the Norman invaders. When William's men attacked, Hereward managed to escape.

What were the Crusades?

SINCE THE SEVENTH CENTURY, MANY ARABS HAD FOLLOWED THE teaching of the Muslim prophet Muhammad. Jerusalem was a city holy to both Muslims and Christians, and when it came under Muslim control it became impossible for Christian pilgrims to visit. Jerusalem was defended by the Seljuk Turks, who considered fighting Christians a holy duty. In 1095, Pope Urban II declared war on the Muslims and ordered the Christians to recapture Jerusalem. Many Christian knights headed for the Holy Land to fight what became known as the Crusades. They lasted from 1095 to 1291.

Who fought in the Crusades?
The Crusades were fought by knights from the aristocratic families of Europe. But the First Crusade was also joined by some 20,000 peasants, led by a fanatical preacher called Peter the Hermit. Most of these peasants were massacred, but the knights were more successful. They captured Jerusalem on July 15, 1099.

Did the crusaders go straight home?
No, the rich knights who fought in the First Crusade set up three new kingdoms in the Holy Land. They ruled over them just like they would a big estate in Europe, collecting taxes from the local people and hiring out land to Arab lords.

Who had the heart of a lion?
Richard I, who was a descendant of William the Conqueror, ruled England from 1189 to 1199. Although he was born in England, he spoke mostly in French. Many English people called him the 'absent king' because he only ever spent six months of his reign in England. The rest of the time he was away fighting – either in France, or in the Holy Land during the Crusades. His bravery while trying to capture the city of Jerusalem earned him the nickname, Coeur de Lion, or Lionheart.

Knights look down on one of the castles built by the Crusaders in the Holy Land.

HOLY KNIGHTS FIGHT CRUSADES

The Crusades were dominated by two orders of knights – who were also monks! These were the Knights Templar and the Hospitallers Of St John. Both orders had castles, forts and hospitals scattered throughout Europe and the Holy Land. They used them to nurse sick pilgrims, train knights and raise money for the Crusades.

How did crusaders attack towns?

WHILE LAYING A SIEGE ON A TOWN, THE CRUSADERS SOMETIMES BUILT huge wooden catapults called mangonels and petrarias. With these, they launched enormous boulders, each of which could kill twenty men at a time.

How did crusaders square-up for a fight?
Crusaders usually fought on horseback, wearing chain mail to protect them from swords and arrows. When surrounded, the knights would dismount and form a large square with their precious horses safely in the centre.

How did the Turks fight during a battle?
The Turks would rush into battle on horseback, fire a volley of arrows, and retreat immediately. It was a tactic that gradually wore down their opponents. If a knight was well protected by armour, the Turks would often shoot his horse instead.

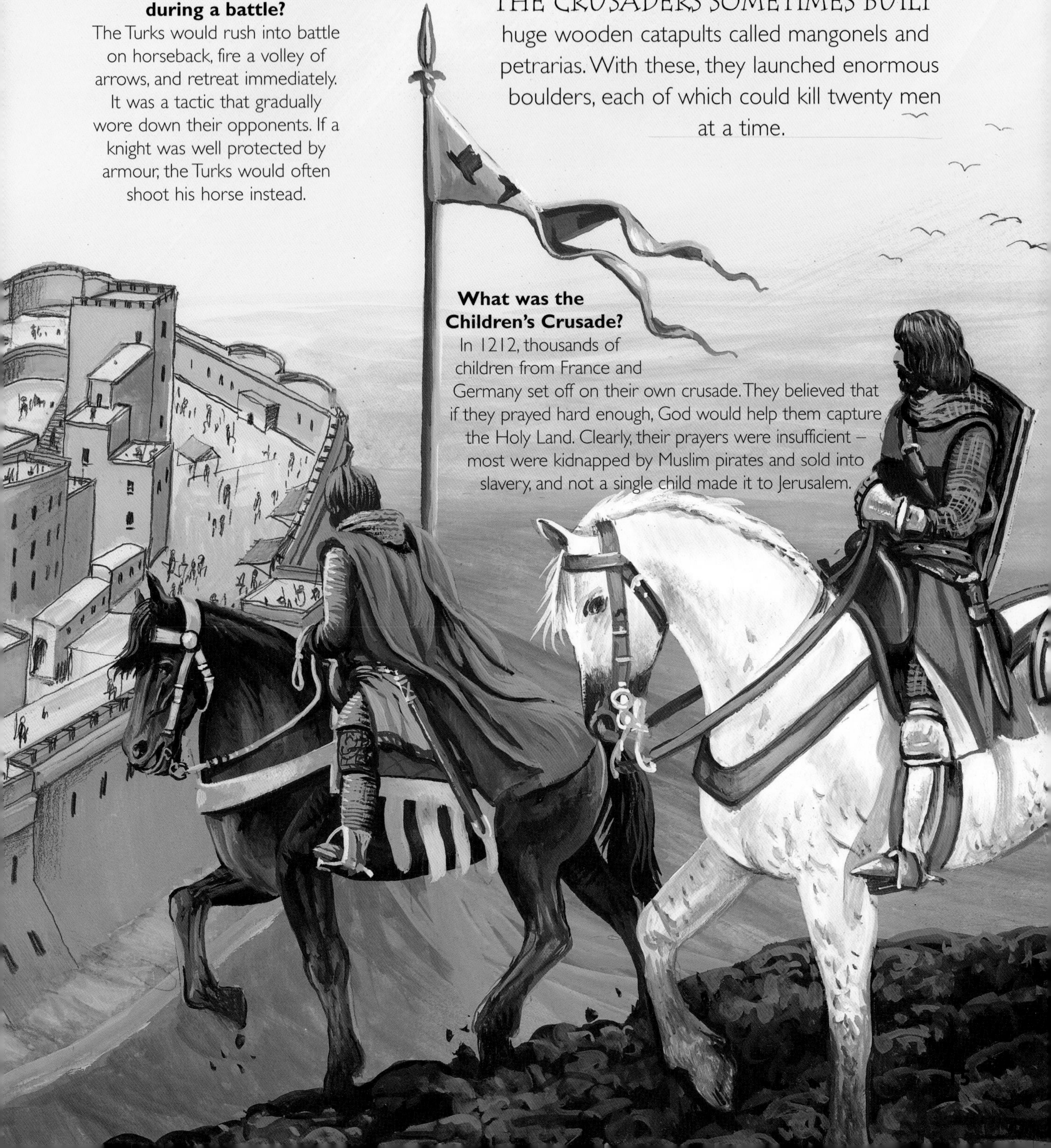

What was the Children's Crusade?
In 1212, thousands of children from France and Germany set off on their own crusade. They believed that if they prayed hard enough, God would help them capture the Holy Land. Clearly, their prayers were insufficient – most were kidnapped by Muslim pirates and sold into slavery, and not a single child made it to Jerusalem.

How did a riding accident unsettle Scotland?

FOR MOST OF THE THIRTEENTH CENTURY, THE PEOPLE OF SCOTLAND WERE AT peace with the English. Under their own ruler, Alexander III, the Scots enjoyed a golden age. But in 1286 poor Alexander died in a riding accident, leaving Scotland with no heir to the throne. Unable to decide who should be their next king, the Scots asked Edward I, king of England, to choose for them. There were two contenders – John Balliol and Robert the Bruce, Lord of Annandale.

Did Balliol betray Scotland?
Edward I chose John Balliol to be the next king of Scotland, because he secretly hoped that he would help England to invade and conquer the Scots. When Balliol was crowned in 1292, he was made to swear allegiance to England. But Balliol would not betray his new kingdom, and made a secret deal with the French to help him conquer northern England. Edward I lost his patience and in 1296 he decided to invade Scotland.

Who was Toom Tabard?
Marching up to Scotland with his army, Edward I massacred some 20,000 people on the borders. No one was spared, not even women and children. The Scottish army was routed at Dunbar and John Balliol surrendered. He was stripped of his royal insignia and became known as Toom Tabard – which means Empty Jacket.

What were the Ragman Rolls?
Every Scottish nobleman was forced to swear allegiance to the king of England. They had to sign a document known as the 'Ragman Rolls'. English people were put into positions of power around Scotland, and it seemed the Scots had lost their independence.

Was it wise to insult William Wallace?
Not really. When the young Scot William Wallace was studying with monks in Dundee, the son of the English governor insulted him. Wallace promptly drew his sword and killed him. Five years later, the English sheriff of Lanark murdered Wallace's wife – and he too paid with his life. Wallace then fled to a nearby forest, where he was joined by Scots eager to expel the English from their homeland.

What happened at Stirling?
The forces of Edward I and William Wallace met at Stirling on September 11, 1297. The English outnumbered the Scots three to one, but the Scots knew the countryside around Stirling very well. Wallace's warriors rushed from hiding to surprise the English troops as they were crossing a narrow bridge over the River Forth, and won an amazing victory.

William Wallace fights at the Battle of Stirling.

How was Wallace buried in four places?
Wallace was made the guardian of Scotland, but in 1298 his forces were defeated by the English at the Battle of Falkirk. Wallace was finally captured in 1305 and taken to the Tower of London. He was hung, drawn and quartered – and the four parts of his body were sent to Berwick, Newcastle, Perth and Stirling.

Why won't Scots kill spiders?
In 1306, Robert the Bruce was in exile and the English had seized his castles. According to legend, as he lay down in despair he watched a spider try six times to swing across a gap and finish its web. The Bruce had himself fought six battles without success. When the spider succeeded at the seventh attempt, the Bruce swore to return to Scotland and fight on. Spiders now hold a special place in Scottish hearts!

What happened at Bannockburn?
At Bannockburn, on July 24, 1314, the Bruce lured the English forces of Edward II on to marshy ground, and defeated them once and for all. In 1328, Scotland finally achieved independence from England when the Treaty of Northampton was signed. The Bruce was crowned king but died a year later.

Robert the Bruce watches a spider complete its web.

Who was the Bruce?

ROBERT THE BRUCE WAS BROUGHT UP AT THE COURT OF EDWARD I, AND his loyalty wavered between the English and his Scottish origins. In 1306, he was crowned king of Scotland by his supporters and war broke out between Scotland and England. By 1314, nearly the whole of Scotland was in his hands.

SCONE STONE GONE

Scottish kings were crowned while sitting on the Stone of Scone, or Stone of Destiny. Nobody knows where this slab of black stone decorated with a cross came from. Some say it was carved in the Middle East, others that it was made by Scottish craftsmen. In 1296, the sacred relic was taken by Edward I. It was not returned to the Scots until 1996. But some people still believe the Scots had tricked Edward I by giving him a false stone!

Richard de Clare, known as Strongbow, became king of Leinster in 1171.

Which king was thrown out for eloping?
Ireland was ruled by a number of 'high kings', and in 1166 they got together to expel Dermot MacMurrough, who was high king of Leinster. He was thrown out for eloping with the daughter of one of the other kings! King Henry II of England saw this as an opportunity to conquer Ireland, and helped MacMurrough to raise an army to attack the high kings and win back his kingdom. MacMurrough was then expected to swear allegiance to the English throne.

What is Castle Hall?
The high kings of Ireland were horrified when Strongbow, a Norman, claimed the throne of Leinster. They refused to give him his inheritance, and Strongbow appealed to Henry II for help. Henry sent his army across the Irish Sea, conquered Ireland and gave Leinster to Strongbow. Then he set up the centre of English rule at Castle Hall in Dublin, and awarded the rest of the land to Norman nobles.

Who was Strongbow?

STRONGBOW WAS THE NICKNAME OF RICHARD DE CLARE, A LONG-legged Norman knight who offered to help MacMurrough win back his throne. He helped him to conquer Dublin in 1170, and to win back the throne of Leinster. Strongbow then married MacMurrough's daughter Aoife. When MacMurrough died in 1171, the long-legged knight inherited his throne and all his wealth and power.

ARMY SPREADS BLACK DEATH

During the 1340s, a terrible army marched across Europe, leaving one in three people dead. It was not an army of soldiers, but an army of rats. The rodents carried a horrific disease called the Black Death. People who were infected started coughing up blood. Red bruises appeared on their skin and lumps as big as tennis balls grew in their armpits. Most died within three days. A lucky few died within hours.

Who improved Irish farming?

AFTER THE CONQUEST OF DUBLIN IN 1170, MANY NORMANS STARTED settling in Ireland. They introduced better farming methods to the Irish countryside, and the country prospered. By 1250, the Irish were exporting food and importing luxury goods like wine and wool.

What did the Normans think of Irish customs?
They liked them so much that they began to adopt them for themselves. They started to speak Irish and took Irish names, and the more Irish they became the more their loyalty to England waned.

Who was Edward the Bruce?
Edward the Bruce was the brother of Robert, and was summoned to Ireland to help the Irish expel the Normans from their land. The people, including some Norman families who now considered themselves to be Irish, welcomed him with open arms.

Why did the Irish starve?
Edward the Bruce was crowned king of Ireland, and led an army of Scots and Irish into battle against the English. In 1318, he was defeated and killed at Dundalk. By now, Ireland was starving as many fields and crops had been burned during the fighting, but English power had been weakened beyond repair.

Who was banned from being Irish?
In 1366, the English king Edward III drew up the Statutes of Kilkenny. Under these laws, English people in Ireland were forbidden to take part in Irish customs or to use the Irish language. Marriages between Irish and English people were also banned.

Who lost their heads?
Edward III gave the English permission to chop off the head of any Irishman they suspected of stealing from them. Despite such behaviour, or perhaps because of it, English influence on Ireland continued to dwindle.

Who was beyond the Pale?
By 1400, England controlled only one twentieth of Ireland. A century later, this had shrunk even further to a narrow strip of land around Dublin. This land was known as the English Pale.

An Irish farmer harvests his crops.

Did the Hundred Years' War last that long?

THE HUNDRED YEARS' WAR WAS A SERIES OF BATTLES BETWEEN THE KINGS AND knights of England and France that lasted from 1337 to 1453 – a total of 116 years. In 1328, Charles IV of France died without leaving an heir. King Edward III of England claimed he should have the French throne. He was descended from an earlier French king and he already ruled Gascony in France. But Philip the Strong was given the French crown, and in 1337 he also seized Gascony. Edward and his knights sailed for France and the Hundred Years' War began.

Which farmers went to war?
The English army included many Welsh and English farmers. During peacetime, they were paid to do military training, and were punished if they did not train enough. During wartime, their pay increased dramatically and they received rations for food and clothing.

What kind of weapons made the English famous?
During the Hundred Years' War, English archers became famous for their deadly use of the longbow. Originally used for hunting in Wales, the longbow took years of practice to master.

How many horses did a knight have?
The richer a knight was, the more horses he had. But every knight, even the poorest one, needed to have at least two. One, called a palfrey, was used for riding around the countryside and hunting. The other, known as a destrier, was the precious war-horse reserved for battle.

Which horses were the best?
The horses of Normandy were believed to be the best in the world. A knight's horse was considered his most precious possession, and the knights of France and England favoured the horses of Normandy above all others.

Henry V at the Battle of Agincourt in 1415.

Edward, the Black Prince, fighting in his famous black armour.

Who was known as the Black Prince?
The most famous knight of the Hundred Years' War was Prince Edward, son of Edward III. He led the English to victory at the Battle of Crécy in 1346 –when he was only sixteen! Edward became known as the Black Prince because he fought in a magnificent suit of black armour.

Did people live long in Medieval times?

IN A TIME WHEN WAR WAS CONSTANTLY BEING FOUGHT, DISEASE WAS RIFE, and medicine was basic to say the least. People were considered old when they got to their forties. Fifty was thought very old. If you lived to be seventy, you were thought to be ... lucky!

Whose wedding brought England and France together?
Henry V became king of England in 1413, and two years later defeated the forces of the French king Charles VI at the famous Battle of Agincourt. Because Henry was partly French, Charles later declared him heir to the French throne. Henry married Charles's daughter, and the French and English royal families were united.

How did the Hundred Years' War end?
In 1422, both Henry V and Charles VI died. Henry's son was too young to rule, and when they realized that the English had no able leader the French took full advantage. They resumed hostilities and by 1453 had expelled the English from France once and for all.

WOMAN BURNT AS WITCH

A French peasant called Joan of Arc believed God had called her to save France from the English. She led an army to the city of Orleans, which the English had been attacking for five months. Dressed in a suit of white armour, she commanded an amazing French victory. Joan was later captured and burnt at the stake as a witch. Centuries after her death, she was made a saint.

Joan of Arc.

What was the Spanish Armada?

THE ARMADA WAS A GROUP OF SOME 130 SHIPS THAT KING PHILIP II OF Spain sent as an invasion force to conquer England in 1588. The term 'armada' simply means 'fleet'. The Spanish were so proud of their fleet that they called it the 'Grande Armada', meaning the big fleet. Some of them were even prouder, and called it the 'Invincible Armada'. Unfortunately for them, it wasn't!

King Philip II of Spain.

Why did Philip II want to conquer England?

Since Elizabeth I became queen in 1558, England had followed the Protestant religion. Under Philip II Spain was a Catholic nation. Philip considered it his holy duty to free England from its Protestant rulers and restore it to the arms of the Roman Catholic Church. He was also fed up with English ships attacking Spanish vessels and robbing them of their loot!

What did Elizabeth do to Catholics?

Elizabeth made life very difficult for English Catholics, particularly in time of war. They were fined if they refused to attend services in Protestant churches. Those that secretly attended mass in Catholic churches ran the risk of imprisonment and possibly death.

What was Philip II like?

Philip II came to the throne of Spain in 1556, at the age of twenty-eight. He was a devout man, who spent a lot of time praying and fasting in his magnificent palace outside Madrid called El Escorial.

English ships attack the Spanish Armada.

Who had bad indigestion?
As a prince, Philip II married Queen Mary of England in a bid to strengthen links between Spain and England. After Mary died in 1588, Philip became an increasingly bitter man. In later life he suffered a disease brought on by eating too many rich foods, and had terrible trouble sleeping.

What were zebras?
Small vessels called zebras were used to carry messages around the Armada, from one ship to another. They also acted as spying ships, galloping ahead of the main fleet to scout for enemy vessels.

Who singed the king's beard?
In 1587, the ships of the Armada were anchored in the Spanish port of Cadiz. Sir Francis Drake, one of Elizabeth's finest captains, set some old ships on fire and steered them into the port – where they set light to many Spanish ships. Drake laughingly called this 'singeing the King of Spain's beard'.

What did the Armada carry?
As well as cannons and arms, the Armada's ships had to carry enormous quantities of food and water. Some ships carried horses and mules, and had large tents on board to shelter the many soldiers who would lead the invasion of England.

Did the Armada conquer England?

NO. OF THE 130 SHIPS THAT SET SAIL FROM LISBON, ONLY 60 EVER RETURNED to Spanish ports. Some had been sunk by the English fleet as they struggled through the English Channel. Others were wrecked by storms on the rocky shores of Ireland and Scotland as they tried to escape. Some 20,000 men lost their lives in the attempt to conquer England.

Queen Elizabeth I of England.

How did the Spanish leaders take the news?
The ragged remnants of the Armada arrived home with the sailors and soldiers dying of starvation and horrible diseases. The fleet's commander Medina Sedonia returned safely but died soon after, a broken man. It is said, on the other hand, that King Philip II received the news of his loss with the calm of a true king.

NUMBER ONE ENEMY KNIGHTED

Francis Drake received permission from Elizabeth I to plunder Spanish ships returning to Europe from the Americas. His pirate raids brought the queen enormous quantities of gold, silver, spices and other treasures. This made him the number one enemy of Spain, and when Elizabeth knighted Drake the Spanish ambassador was red with rage.

Who were the Pilgrim Fathers?

ON AUGUST 5, 1620, A GROUP OF 102 MEN AND WOMEN SAILED FROM Southampton, England, in search of a new and better life in America. Their arrival and settlement in what is now New England was part of a movement across the Atlantic that had begun in 1607. Thirty-five of the group followed a religion called the English Separatist Church. They went to America to escape religious persecution. As a result, the whole group that left England in 1620 came to be known as the Pilgrim Fathers.

What ship did the pilgrims sail on?
The pilgrims travelled on a small ship called the *Mayflower*. Only twenty-seven metres long, it was a craft built to travel close to the coast of Europe, not to cross an ocean. Its passengers suffered terribly during the journey, as they were jammed together in close quarters and hurled about by rough seas.

Who had a brief glimpse of America?
One of the pilgrims, a woman called Dorothy Bradford, fell overboard and drowned just after she first gazed at the coast of America.

Why were the pilgrims off course?

The captain of the ship was aiming to land in Virginia, which already had English settlements. But strong winds blew the *Mayflower* off course and it was forced to anchor at a bay in Cape Cod, Massachusetts. The pilgrims named it Plymouth Bay, after Plymouth Sound in England where their voyage had begun.

How did the pilgrims survive?

The Pilgrim Fathers reached America in December 1620, a harsh time of year to start a colony. They built huts to shelter from the freezing weather, then searched desperately for food. Luckily, local Native Americans came to their aid and taught them the skills they needed to survive.

How did the Native Americans help?

The Native Americans showed the settlers how to hunt and trap. They taught them how to make maple sugar, how to sew warm moccasins for their feet, and how to build canoes.

Who was John Smith?

AN ADVENTURER, SAILOR AND SOLDIER OF FORTUNE, CAPTAIN JOHN Smith became the leader of the Virginia settlement. He was captured by Algonquians, and taken to a place called Werowocomoco. The Algonquians held a great feast in his honour, but then a group of warriors grabbed Smith. He was saved only when a chief's daughter named Pocahontas begged for his life.

Who celebrated Thanksgiving?

In 1621, the Pilgrims harvested their first crops. To celebrate, they caught and cooked birds then found only in America – turkeys! The feast would become an annual celebration called Thanksgiving, which is still a very important date in the American calendar.

Were the pilgrims the first English in America?

No. In April 1607, three ships had reached the east coast of America, and anchored at Chesapeake Bay, Virginia. The colonists on board had built a settlement which they called Jamestown after King James I, ruler of England and Scotland.

Who were the Algonquians?

Some of the Native Americans that helped the English settlers survive belonged to the Algonquian nation. They lived around the rivers of Virginia, hunting and growing crops. They happily traded with the settlers, exchanging food and furs for tools.

Pilgrims make their way ashore at Plymouth Bay in what is now Massachusetts, USA.

What was the Jacobite Rebellion?

IN 1707, ENGLAND AND SCOTLAND JOINED TOGETHER UNDER THE Act of Union to form Great Britain. The first king of the new union was George I, who was a Protestant and a member of the Hanover family. The Hanovers were German, and George barely spoke English. Many Catholics, especially those in Scotland, believed members of the Stuart family had a stronger claim to the throne. Matters came to a head in an uprising called the Jacobite Rebellion.

Who was the Young Pretender?
Bonnie Prince Charlie, the son of James Edward Stuart, was known as the Young Pretender. He was born and educated in Rome, but the Jacobites hoped that he would come to claim the British throne. In July 1745, he landed in Scotland with only seven followers and said: 'I am come home'.

What did the Scots think of Charlie?
Bonnie Prince Charlie was a hero to the Scottish people even when he was still living abroad. They had written songs and poems about him, and placed their hopes in him. When he landed in Scotland, people rushed from the Highlands to fight with him for the British throne.

Who was the Old Pretender?
James Edward Stuart was known as the Old Pretender because he 'pretended to', or claimed, the English throne. The word Jacobite comes from the Latin for James. The Old Pretender was helped to lead a rebellion against George I by the French king, Louis XIV, who was also a Catholic. But the Jacobite Rebellion of 1715 was crushed.

What weapons did the highlanders use?
Highland warriors used long, two-handed swords called claymores. They also had short daggers called dirks. During a battle they would protect themselves with small shields called torges.

Scottish Highlanders in battle against the Duke of Cumberland's troops. at Culloden.

What happened at Culloden?
Culloden was one of the bloodiest battles fought on British soil. On April 16, 1746, an English army led by George II's son, the Duke of Cumberland, met Bonnie Prince Charlie's followers on Culloden Moor. Charlie's Highlanders were freezing and exhausted from their long march, and over 1,000 of them were massacred.

Who was the Butcher?
The Duke of Cumberland became known as the Butcher. To make sure the Jacobites never tried to invade England again, he decided to wipe out the Highlanders. All the men left on the battlefield of Culloden were slaughtered.

Who had their bagpipes banned?
After Culloden, Highlanders were forbidden to use tartan, wear kilts, or carry guns. They were not even allowed to play their bagpipes. Most were evicted from their houses and many emigrated to Canada in search of a better life. That is why there are so many Canadians of Scottish descent.

Bonnie Prince Charlie.

PRINCE DRESSES AS MAID

Bonnie Prince Charlie escaped from the slaughter at Culloden, but £30,000 was offered for his capture. Despite the size of the reward, nobody betrayed him. The Young Pretender finally escaped by disguising himself as the maid of a Scot named Flora Macdonald, and pretending to have the name Betty Burke!

Who was a long way from home?

BY SEPTEMBER 1745, BONNIE PRINCE CHARLIE HAD GATHERED enough followers to march on England. They defeated the English at Prestonpans, and scored another victory at Falkirk. But as the Jacobites reached Derby in England, they started to falter. Far from home, they missed the support of their people.

What was the British Raj?

A Britsh Army soldier in India.

THE WORD RAJ IS INDIAN FOR REIGN OR RULE. AS BRITISH TRADERS MADE more money, so Britain began to conquer parts of India. Some territories were conquered by force, like the Raj of Berar which was home to five million people and countless treasures. A few kingdoms remained independent, but they were ruled by Indian princes who were protected by the British. In 1783 the East India Company started running the administration of India on behalf of the British government. This began a period of rule known as the British Raj.

What was the East India Company?

As far back as 1693, a British company called the East India Company was controlling trade between India and the rest of the British Empire. It made large amounts of money by trading in goods like gold, silk and precious stones. It also made the British government lots of money by collecting taxes. By 1767, the East India Company was paying the government £400,000 a year. The company was the main driving force behind the British conquest of lands in Asia.

How did life change in India?

The British saw themselves as the rulers of India. English replaced Persian as the language of government. In 1853, the first Indian railway was built. But such things had little impact on most of India's 200 million inhabitants, who continued to live traditional village lives.

What did missionaries do?

Christian missionaries were allowed to teach and preach to the Indians. But the Indian population already had strong religious beliefs. Most people were Hindus, and most of the others were Muslims.

What upset the Indian people?

The removal of many local princes caused great alarm. The British also took away a lot of land, and introduced heavy taxes. But worst of all, Indian soldiers suspected that the British were trying to convert them to Christianity.

Was the British Army all British?

BY 1857, 40,000 BRITISH SOLDIERS WERE STATIONED IN THE INDIAN REGION.

But the army also contained 200,000 Asians. They had joined up because they received regular pay and enjoyed better working conditions than most Indians.

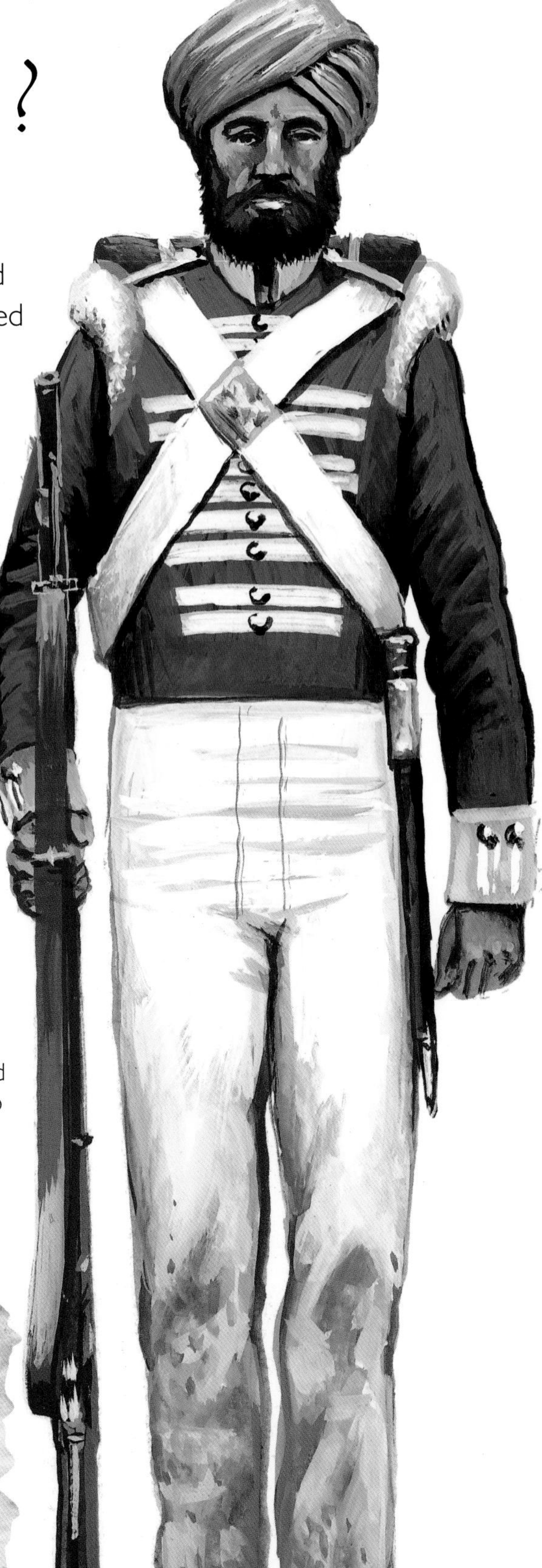

An Indian soldier in the British Army.

How did cows and pigs start a rebellion?

In 1857, Indian soldiers known as sepoys were given new rifles to use. To load them, soldiers had to bite the ends off cartridges which they believed were sealed with cow and pig fat. This horrified all the sepoys. The Hindus believed cows were sacred and the Muslims believed pigs were unclean. When British officers ignored their complaints, the sepoys mutinied.

What cities were captured in the Sepoy Mutiny?

The sepoys took Meerut and Cawnpore, and captured Delhi and Lucknow after long sieges. They proclaimed a local ruler called Bahadur Shah the emperor of all India. It looked as if Britain would lose the jewel of its empire. But the outnumbered British rallied and somehow restored their rule.

Did things get better for the Indians?

The Sepoy Mutiny came as a big shock to the British, who had been hopelessly ignorant of Indian discontent. English people were forbidden to seize any more Indian land after the mutiny. New laws were also passed giving Indians the right to practise their religions and customs.

Who became civil servants?

In 1858, the East India Company was abolished and a special ministry was set up in London to look after India. Many Indians were now given jobs in the civil service.

GREAT SOUL BRINGS INDEPENDENCE

The Indians did not gain independence from Britain until 1947, following the efforts of a leader named Mahatma (which means 'great soul') Gandhi. He hated violence and taught his followers to protest peacefully. Gandhi went on hunger strikes and was frequently arrested, but was rewarded when India gained independence.

What was the 'Scramble for Africa'?

BY THE LATTER HALF OF THE NINETEENTH CENTURY, MANY EUROPEAN countries had become industrialized. They looked to Africa as a source of raw materials and a market for their goods. This started the 'Scramble for Africa' – a time when European nations conquered different parts of Africa and turned them into colonies. By the late 1800s, nearly the whole of Africa had been carved up between the European powers.

Which parts of Africa did Britain colonize?
Between 1882 and 1902, Britain laid claim to countries including Egypt, Rhodesia (now Zimbabwe), Nyasaland (now Malawi), Uganda, Kenya, Ashanti (now Ghana) and Nigeria. The colonies provided England with raw materials such as wood, rubber and timber. Gold could also be obtained from West Africa, while the mines of South Africa were rich in diamonds.

Who invaded Zululand?
In 1879, a British army under the command of Lieutenant General Frederick Augustus Thesiger, Earl of Chelmsford, invaded Zululand, a country in south-east Africa. But they met ferocious resistance from the armies of a people called Zulus.

Boers – Dutch settlers – in southern Africa. They fought against the invading British to protect the lands they had settled.

Who won the Battle of Khambula

THE BRITISH WERE WELL PREPARED, AND WELL ARMED WITH CANNONS AND shotguns. As the Zulus started to close their pincer movement, the British unleashed a hail of bullets. Over 3,000 Zulus lost their lives that night while the British lost only thirty-two soldiers.

Who was outnumbered at Khambula?

On March 29, 1789 several hundred British soldiers led by Colonel H E Wood were attacked by 25,000 Zulus at a place called Khambula. The Zulus employed their famous 'horns of the beast' movement, advancing on Wood's men who were stationed in a carefully chosen spot on top of a hill.

What did the Zulus chant at the British?

As they neared the British troops, the Zulus taunted them. They called out 'Don't run away, Johnny, we want to talk to you. We're the boys from Ishandlwana.'

What did the Zulus do at Ishandlwana?

The Zulus surprised the British at a mountain named Ishandlwana on January 21, 1879. Under the guidance of their leader Cetshwayo, the Zulus destroyed a British regiment.

British soldiers firing a Maxim gun.

What were the horns of the beast?

Zulu warriors used a traditional method of attack called the 'horns of the beast'. Two regiments, representing the beasts' horns, moved in a pincer movement around the side of the enemy. More regiments, representing the belly of the beast, then moved in to crush anyone in their way.

What happened to the Zulus?

The terrible defeat at Khambula turned the tide of war against Cetshwayo and his brave warriors. They kept on fighting the British, but their pride had been broken and they fought out of despair for their homeland. In 1906, the last Zulu revolt was crushed.

ZAMBEZI TREASURE UP FOR GRABS

In 1888, an African king called Lobengula escaped from advancing British troops with a hoard of treasure including gold, diamonds and ivory. The king hid his loot somewhere on the banks of the Zambezi River, but died before he could return to claim it. Some say it is still hidden there, waiting for someone to find it.

Index

AB

CDE

FGH

IJKL

MN

OPQR

STU

VWXYZ